If you can't explain it simply,

you don't understand it well enough.

Albert Einstein

to my Family.

Learn
JavaScript
VISUALLY

Ivelin Demirov

2014

{iv} Credits & Legal

AUTHOR
Ivelin Demirov

EDITOR
John Duncan

PAGE DESIGN
Jordan Milev

ILLUSTRATOR
Ivelin Demirov

PROOFREADER
Carol Dew

CREDITS
A book is a collaborative affair and it takes so many people to make it a reality and I would like to thank every **Kickstarter backer** who has helped to prepare this book for production.

I must acknowledge the help of the online JavaScript community, who have toiled in the background for many years to help make JavaScript the exciting programming language it has become

ISBN-13
9780993836701

CONTACTS
jsvisually.com

{v} About this book.

THE PROBLEM

People cannot be blamed for thinking programming is hard when trying it out for the first time. Learning to program is like learning a new language.

A number of rules and grammar syntax guidelines exist to follow. It also requires memorizing a bevy of glossary terms for each language, and unless a person works with programming at least 8 hours a day, the person is unlikely to become very familiar with programming quickly; at least, that has been the situation for years until now.

THE METHODOLOGY

The approach involves teaching programming by recognizing common characters via simple illustrations.

The visual approach works because it is one of the most fundamental ways of learning. Everyone as a baby and toddler learns the world around them via sight and sound long before there is comprehension associated with letters and meanings.

Programming works in modules and building blocks. As a person learns a few basic modules and steps, he can then learn to build more complex modules on those first basic units.

It's a building block approach where bigger structures can be coded once the basic modules are mastered. I start with a set of basic building blocks that are easy to learn through illustrations and metaphors.

From there, a user can apply multiple variations and build further. However, the initial set of building blocks becomes a Rosetta stone of sorts, allowing a user to program and build in any situation going forward.

{vi} Table of Contents.

1. Why JavaScript?

JavaScript is the

Most Important
Most Popular
Easy To Learn
Functional
Dynamically Typed
Object Oriented
Scripting
Client Side
Server Side

Language Of The Web

JavaScript can be inserted between
<head> and *</head>* and/or *<body>* and *</body>* tags

```
1  <html>
2    <head>
3      <title>My title</title>
4      <script>alert("It's best if I sit low!");</script>        <!-- embed script -->
5    </head>
6    <body>
7      <h1>Where do I put JavaScript?</h1>
8  <!--lines 4 and 9 create a pop up with a message-->
9      <script src = "main.js"></script>                          <!-- external script -->
10   </body>
11 </html>
```
index.html

```
1    alert("I pop-up from the external file!");
```
main.js

3.EXERCISE:
Where do I put JavaScript?

PROBLEM: Write a simple HTML file and link a *javascript.js* file with it.

YOUR CODE: *Write your code here and compare it with the answer below*

```
1
2
3
4
5
6
7
8
```

ANSWER: *Use a QR code reader from a smart phone or tablet to see the answer*

Small bits of JavaScript can be tested right in your browser.
In the **developer tools** open the JavaScript *console.*

in the console enter 2+2 and hit Enter

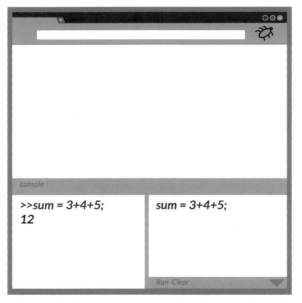

install the Firebug extension for even more control

click the red arrow to open/close the code panel

5.EXERCISE:
Practice JavaScript.

PROBLEM:

Open the console of your browser and calculate the area of the right triangle below

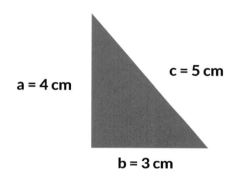

a = 4 cm

c = 5 cm

b = 3 cm

YOUR CODE:

```
1
2
3
4
5
6
7
8
```

ANSWER:

An Interpreter/compiler is a computer software that interprets/compiles and executes code. JavaScript can be interpreted or compiled.

Most modern browsers compile the code before execution

I am Private JS.
I will read, interpret/compile and execute your commands
from top to bottom and from left to right

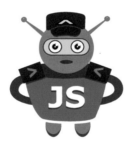

I will run everything between the <script> tags

```
1   <script>
2       alert("This line first");
3       //ignore this line. It's a comment
4       alert("This line second");
5   </script>
```

index.html

7.EXERCISE:
The Interpreter/Compiler.

PROBLEM:

Modify the code to change the order of execution to the following:
first
second
third

```
1    alert("execute this second");
2    alert("execute this first");
3    alert("execute this third");
```

YOUR CODE:

```
1
2
3
```

ANSWER:

Are used to *separate* statements. Optional, but a good practice.

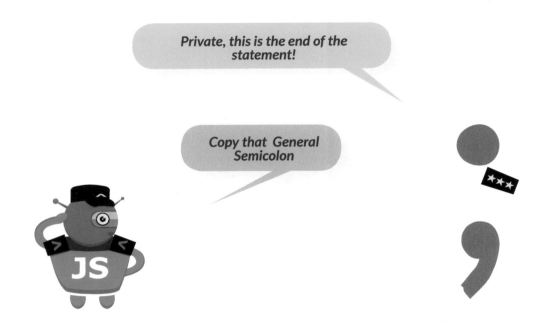

Missing a semicolon might not give you an error, but your code might not run as expected

```
1   //the first semicolon is required when statements are in one line
2   x = 2; y = 6
3
4   //the line break acts like a semicolon
5   x = 2
6   y = 6
7
8   //the interpreter will see: x = 8;
9   x
10  =
11  8
12
13  //Oops, we have a problem. The interpreter will see: return; true;
14  return
15  true;
```

9.EXERCISE:
Semicolons.

PROBLEM:

Add the missing semicolons.

```
1    x = 2 y = 3
2    z = x + y
```

YOUR CODE:

```
1
2
3
```

ANSWER:

```
item = group[ (current.index + i ) % len ];
```

```
coming.c

F._after
```

Are *grouping symbols* which are always in pairs.

Brackets:
hold arrays

```
1    //array of numbers
2    var num = [1, 2, 3, 4, 5, 6, 7, 8];
3    //array of names
4    var names = ["John", "Paul"];
5    //empty array
6    var myArray = [];
```

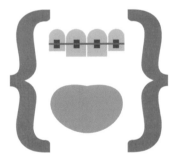

Braces:
create objects
group statements

```
1    //create new object
2    var myObj = {};
3    //group statements
4    var a = function () {
5        alert("statement 1");
6        alert("statement 2");
7    };
```

Parentheses:
supply
parameters

group
expressions

execute
functions

```
1    //supply parameters x and y
2    function myParents (x, y) {
3        return x + y;
4    }
5    //group expressions to control the order
6    //of execution
7    var a = (3 + 2) * 7;      //a = 35
8
9    //execute functions
10   myParents(2, 3);        //5
```

11.EXERCISE:
Brackets. Braces. Parentheses.

PROBLEM:

Change the brackets to braces to resolve the code error.

Don't worry about the meaning yet, just identify the brackets and learn to type and test code.

```
1    var a = function () [
2        alert("statement 1");
3        alert("statement 2");
4    ];
5    SyntaxError
6    a();
```

YOUR CODE:

```
1
2
3
4
5
6
```

ANSWER:

The interpreter *ignores* comments, but they are great to leave important information for us and other coders

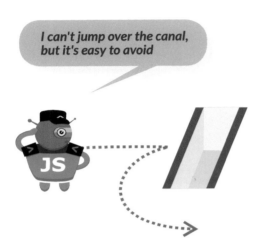

The interpreter will ignore a single line after the // symbols

```
1  <html>
2    <head>
3      <title>Single Comments</title>
4    </head>
5    <body>
6      <script>
7        //one comment per line
8
9      </script>
10   </body>
11 </html>
```

The interpreter will ignore anything in between /* and */

```
1  <html>
2    <head>
3      <title>Multiline Comments</title>
4    </head>
5    <body>
6      <script>
7        /* Long multiline comments
8        are useful for "disabling" some
9        part of your code
10       var = 123;
11       console.log("comments");
12       */
13       /* but are good for single line too */
14
15     </script>
16   </body>
17 </html>
```

13. EXERCISE:
Comments.

PROBLEM:

Comment out the following code in order to disable it from execution

```
1    var myObj = {};
2
3    var a = function () {
4        alert("statement 1");
5        alert("statement 2");
6    };
```

YOUR CODE:

```
1
2
3
4
5
6
```

ANSWER:

Are the kind of *values* manipulated in a program

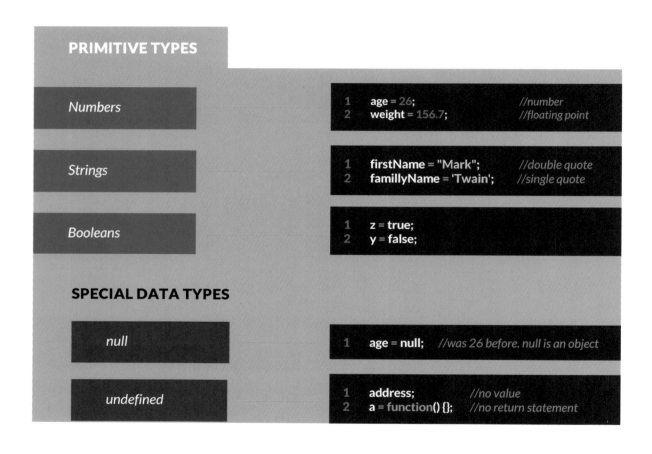

PRIMITIVE TYPES

Numbers

```
1   age = 26;              //number
2   weight = 156.7;        //floating point
```

Strings

```
1   firstName = "Mark";    //double quote
2   famillyName = 'Twain'; //single quote
```

Booleans

```
1   z = true;
2   y = false;
```

SPECIAL DATA TYPES

null

```
1   age = null;    //was 26 before. null is an object
```

undefined

```
1   address;            //no value
2   a = function() {};  //no return statement
```

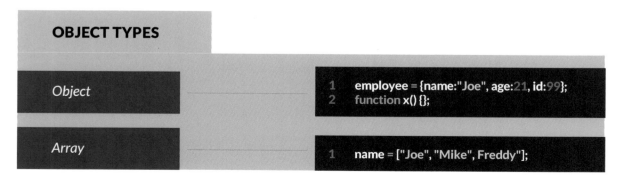

OBJECT TYPES

Object

```
1   employee = {name:"Joe", age:21, id:99};
2   function x() {};
```

Array

```
1   name = ["Joe", "Mike", Freddy"];
```

15.EXERCISE:
Data types.

PROBLEM:

Assign the following to a different letter from the alphabet:

your name,

your age,

you like beer

make a comment with the data type for each one

YOUR CODE:

```
1
2
3
```

ANSWER:

Variables (able to vary) are like *labels* to identify containers with information

empty (undefined) variable declared by the name "box"

null is like a vacuum. It's an object, it's there, but it's nothing

```
1    //this variable is declared with a name but
2    //undefined as value
3    var box;
4    //null is an object
5    var box2 = null;
```

box now has the numeric value of 26

box2 and box3 refer to the same value in memory 24

```
1    //our variables have new values
2    //'box' is now initialized with the number 26,
3    //'box2' is not null anymore
4    var box = 26;
5    var box2 = 24;
```

```
1    //assign the same value to 2 different
2    //variables by separating them with comma
3    var box2 = 24,
4        box3 = 24;
```

Each container can only have one object inside it, but can have many labels on it.

```
1    var name = true;
2    //the last assigned value replaces the previous
3    var name = "John";
4
5    //display the value of variable 'name'
6    console.log(name);
7    //John
```

Variable names (labels) are case sensitive and can only start with a letter (A-Z, a-z), an underscore (_) or $

```
1    //valid variable names:
2    var _myVar = "Yes";
3    var $myVar = "Yes";
4    var my$Var = "Yes";
5    var myVar$ = "Yes";
6    var myVar77 = "Yes";
7    var $myVAR_ = "Yes";
```

17.EXERCISE:
Variables.

PROBLEM:

John is a 25 year old male from United Kingdom.

Assign all we know about him to a different variable so we can use it later.

YOUR CODE:

```
1
2
3
4
5
6
7
```

ANSWER:

Declaration is *reserving* a space in the memory. Put a label on it.
Initialization is the *assignment* of an initial value. Put something in the box.

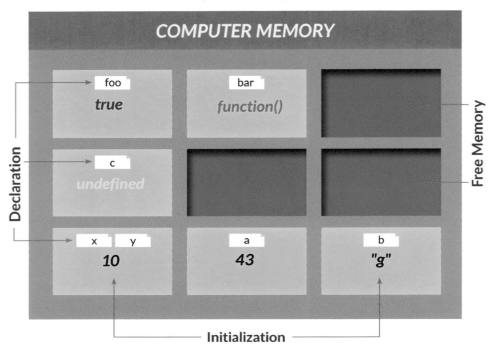

You can think of computer memory as an array of boxes

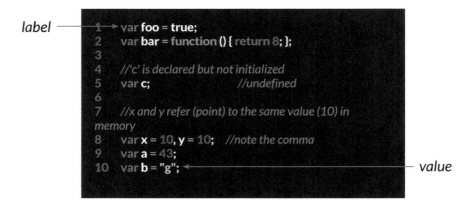

19.EXERCISE:
Declaration and initialization.

PROBLEM:

Declare 5 different variables: **a, b, c, d** and **e**.
Assign a different type of value to each variable.
Leave one variable undefined.

YOUR CODE:

```
1
2
3
4
5
6
7
```

ANSWER:

Operators that require *single* operand

Operand   Operator

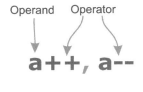

a++, a--   take the value then add/subtract 1

++a, --a   add/subtract 1 then take the value

!a   logical opposite of **a**

+a, -a   positive/negative value of **a**

```
1    var a = 8;
2    console.log(a++);   //8
3
4    var b = 8;
5    console.log(++b);   //9
6
7    var a = true;
8    !a;                 //false
9
10   a = -b;             //attempts to convert b to a number, if its not: returns NaN,
11                       //if it is, negates the value of b and assigns it to a. b retains it's value
12
13   a = +b;             //attempts to convert b to a number, if it's not: returns NaN. b retains its value
```

21.EXERCISE:
Unary operators.

PROBLEM: Using an unary operator, increase the value of a variable **'a'**

OUTPUT: "The value of '**a**' is: 11"

.

YOUR CODE:

```
1
2
3
4
5
6
7
8
```

```
item = group[ (current.index + i ) % len ];
                                              coming.c
                                              F._after
```

Symbols used to operate a value or a variable. Require *two* operands

+, -, *, /, %   Arithmetic Operators

=, *=, /=, %=, +=,-=, <<=, >>=, >>>=, &=, ^=, |=   Assignment Operators

&, |, ^, ~, <<, >>, >>>

                                        Bitwise Operators

==, !=, ===, !==, >, >=, <, <=

                                   Comparison Operators

&&, ||, !   Logical Operators

```
1    //Arithmetic Operators are the same we know from math
2    2 * 3                    //=6  Multiplication
3    4 / 2                    //=2  Division
4    4 + 3                    //=7  Addition
5    4 - 3                    //=1  Subtraction
6    4 % 3                    //=1  Modulus (Division Remainder)
7
8    //Assignment Operators
9    a = b = 2;               //a = 2, b =2
10   a += 2;                  //a = a + 2;
11   a *= 2;                  //a = a * 2;
12
13   //Bitwise Operators
14   a & b;                   //AND
15   a | b;                   //OR
16   a ^ b;                   //XOR
17
18   //Comparison Operators
19   a === b;                 //returns true if the operands are strictly equal
20   a > b;                   //returns true if the left operand is greater than the right operand
```

23.EXERCISE:
Binary operators.

PROBLEM: Add the value of two variables and display the result in the console using console.log() method.

OUTPUT: "8"

YOUR CODE:

```
1
2
3
4
5
6
7
8
```

ANSWER:

24. Bit operations.

Manipulation of bits *(zeros and ones)* by bitwise operators

AND

&	1	0
1	1	0
0	0	0

XOR

∧	1	0
1	0	1
0	1	0

OR

|	1	0
1	1	1
0	1	0

NOT (unary)

~	1	0
	0	1

```
1    //AND
2    1 & 1      //1
3    1 & 0      //0
4    0 & 0      //0
5
6    //OR
7    1 | 1      //1
8    1 | 0      //1
9    0 & 0      //0
```

```
1    //XOR
2    1 ^ 1      //0
3    1 ^ 0      //1
4    0 ^ 0      //0
5
6    //NOT
7    ~1         //-13
8    ~0         //-1
9    ~~123      //123
```

25.EXERCISE:
Bit operators.

PROBLEM: Add the numbers 2 and 3 using a bit operator and display the result in the console using the console.log() method

OUTPUT: "2"

YOUR CODE:

```
1
2
3
4
5
6
7
8
```

ANSWER:

The *order* in which operations are performed

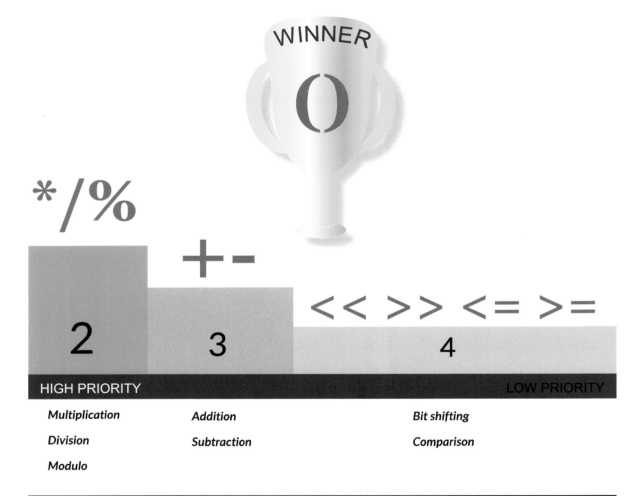

*/%

+-

<< >> <= >=

HIGH PRIORITY		LOW PRIORITY
2	3	4

Multiplication   Addition   Bit shifting

Division   Subtraction   Comparison

Modulo

```
1    //3 *5 is executed first and the result added to 2
2    //the result is 17 (not 25)
3    var precedence = 2 + 3 * 5;
4
5    //we can use parentheses to control the precedence
6    //2+3 is executed first and the result multiplied by 2
7    //the result is 25
8    var precedence2 = (2 + 3) * 5;
```

PROBLEM:

Modify the code so that the result is 10.5

```
1   var result = 33 -12/2;
2   document.write(result);
3   //27
```

YOUR CODE:

```
1
2
3
4
5
6
7
8
```

ANSWER:

Are *commands* to be executed

```
1    //this is one long statement
2    document.getElementById ("bold").innerHTML = "My text";
3
4    //control flow(conditional) statements
5    if (true) {
6        x = 8;      //{ x = 8; } is a block statement
7    }
8    else {
9        x = 6;
10   }
```

JavaScript is case sensitive

```
1    //JavaScript is case sensitive
2    //these variables are completely different
3    var myApple = "red";
4    var myapple = "red";
5    var MyApple = "red";
```

White space

```
1    //JavaScript ignores multiple spaces and tabs
2    //those are the same. The first space is required
3    var whiteSpace="empty";
4    var          whiteSpace          =          "empty";
5    //white spaces are preserved in strings
6    var strings = "preserve     my               format";
```

Code blocks

```
1    //functions are examples  of code blocks
2    //or any group of statements delimited by braces
3    function myFunction() {
4        var a = 3;
5        alert ("my group" + a);
6    }
```

29.EXERCISE:
Statements.

PROBLEM:

Write a statement that has a case sensitive variable name containing a string with many white spaces

YOUR CODE:

```
1
2
3
4
5
6
7
8
```

ANSWER:

Sets of *literals, variables and operators* that resolve to a value.

true

3

4+3

false

"String"

EXPRESSION TYPES

Arithmetic: evaluates to a number
Logical: evaluates to true or false
String: evaluates to a character string
Object: evaluates to an object

```
1   //Arithmetic expression
2   var a = 3;
3
4   //Logical expression
5   var b = true;
6
7   //String expression
8   var c = "String";
9
10  //Object expression
11  var apple = new Apple("Macintosh");
```

31. EXERCISE:
Expressions.

PROBLEM:

Write an expression that represents the perimeter of the rectangle below. The perimeter of any rectangle is the sum of the lengths of its sides.

a = 5

b = 4

YOUR CODE:

```
1
2
3
4
5
6
7
8
```

ANSWER:

Are group of characters *(text)*

" I am just a fancy word for text "

```
1    //A string is just text in quotes
2    //JavaScript uses 2 types of quotes:
3    //single quotes
4    var single = 'Hello JavaScript';
5    //and double quotes
6    var double = "Hello String";
7    //single quotes can be inside double quotes
8    var single = "I'm single quote inside double quotes";
9    //double quotes can be inside single quotes
10   var double = 'This is "double quotes" inside single quotes';
```

With the backslash character, I can escape the quote command.
I'll treat it as a character

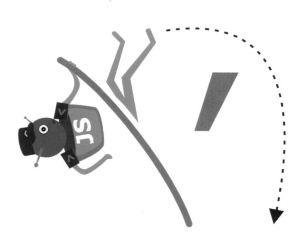

```
1    // Escaping a single quote
2    var escape = 'I\'m escaping';
3    // I'm escaping
4
5    // Escaping a double quote
6    var double = "Hello \"quote\" ";
7    // Hello "quote"
8
9    // \n - new line
10   var newline = "Hello \nWorld!";
11   // Hello
12   // World!
13
14   //unicode special characters
15   var unicode = "\u00A9 All Rights";    // ©
16   // \t - Horizontal tab
17   // \b - Backspace
18   // \r - Carriage return
19   // \\ - Backslash
```

PROBLEM:

Use the console.log() method to display the following message exactly as it appears

```
1   Hello my friend,
2   this message and its meaning
3           was formatted using  "JavaScript'©
```

YOUR CODE:

```
1
2
3
4
5
6
7
8
```

ANSWER:

Is the word for *joining* strings together

cone + cat + ten + ate

```
1   //concatenation of strings
2   var conString = "con" + "cat" + "enate";
3   //the result is: concatenate
```

```
1   //numbers in quotes become strings
2   var a = "1";
3   var b = "2";
4   var c = a + b;
5   //the result is a string: c = "12"
```

```
1   //concatenation is different from addition
2   var a = 1;
3   var b = 2;
4   var c = a + b;
5   //the result is a number: c = 3
```

to me it looks like You forgot the quotes on b, I will treat it as a string

Are You doing math? I will convert the string to number

```
1   //one string, makes everything  string
2   var a = "1";        //this is a string
3   var b = 2;          //this is a number
4   var c = a + b;
5   //The result is a string: c = 12
```

```
1   //concatenation is only when we have "+" sign
2   var a = "3";        //this is a string
3   var b = 2;          //this is a number
4   var c = a * b;
5   //The result is a number: c = 6
```

PROBLEM:

Join "java" and "script" with the number 13.
make sure you have a space before the number.
Print it in the console.

YOUR CODE:

```
1
2
3
4
5
6
7
8
```

ANSWER:

```
item = group[ (current.index + i ) % len ];
```
coming.c

F._after

Do not use as variables, methods or object names

25 words to remember

1	break		1	//reserved for future use
2	case		2	
3	catch		3	class
4	continue		4	const
5	debugger		5	enum
6	default		6	export
7	delete		7	extends
8	do		8	import
9	else		9	super
10	finally		10	
11	for		11	
12	function		12	
13	if		13	//reserved in strict mode
14	in		14	
15	instanceof		15	implements
16	new		16	let
17	return		17	private
18	switch		18	public
19	this		19	yield
20	throw		20	interface
21	try		21	package
22	typeof		22	protected
23	var		23	static
24	void		24	arguments
25	while		25	eval

```
1    //You will get an error if you try to use a reserved word
2    var break = "Error in my code if I use a reserved word";
⊗ 3    SyntaxError: Unexpected token break
```

37.EXERCISE:
Reserved words.

PROBLEM:

Find and correct the error

```
1    //declare some variables
2    var default = "1";
3    var export = "Export Number";
4    var modify = default + " " + export;
```

YOUR CODE:

```
1
2
3
4
5
6
```

ANSWER:

Comparison operators are used to compare(test) two values and return *true* or *false*

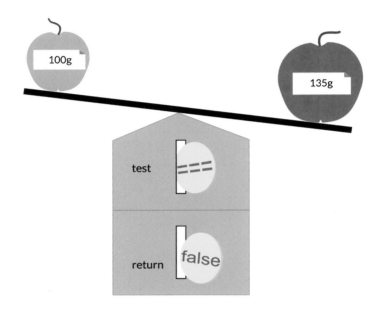

Equal vs Strictly Equal

```
1    var greenApple = 100;
2    var redApple = 135;
3
4    greenApple === redApple;
5    //test if values and the data type are identical
6    //false
7
8    greenApple < redApple;
9    //test if 100 is less than 135
10   //true
11
12   greenApple !== redApple;
13   //test if not identical
14   //true
```

```
1    //Equal
2    //test if values are the same
3    1 == "1";        //true
4
5    //Strictly Equal
6    //test if values and data types are the same
7    1 === "1";       //false
8
```

39.EXERCISE:
Comparisons.

PROBLEM:

Compare the colors of an orange and an apple and display the result in the document

YOUR CODE:

```
1
2
3
4
5
6
7
8
```

ANSWER:

```
item = group[ (current.index + i ) % len ];
```
coming.c

F._after

Conditional statements are used to take *action* based on *decision*

*If it is sunny, I am going to London.
If not, I am going to Paris.*

Condition

if else

```
1    var sunny = true,
2        rainy = false;
3    if (sunny) {           //if true
4        console.log("turn right");
5
6    } else {               //if false
7        console.log("keep straight");
8    }
```

conditional (ternary) operator

```
1    //variable = (condition) ? exp1 : exp2
2    var where = "Paris";
3    where === "London" ? (        //if
4        alert("In 200 meters, "),  //comma
5        alert("turn right")
6    ) : (                          //else
7        console.log("please"),     //this is printed
8        console.log("turn left")
9    );
```

if elseif else

```
1    var sunny = true,
2        rainy = false;
3    if (rainy) {           //if true
4        console.log("keep straight");
5
6    } else if (sunny) {    //if true
7        console.log("turn right");
8
9    } else {               //if false
10       console.log("turn left");
11   }
```

switch

```
1    var where = "London";
2    switch(where)
3    {
4    case "London":    //if true
5        console.log("turn right");
6        break;
7    case "Paris":     //if true
8        console.log("keep straight");
9        break;
10   default:          //if false
11       console.log("turn left");
12   }
```

41.EXERCISE:
Conditions.

PROBLEM:

Private JS wonders what is the distance from Fremont, CA to San Jose, CA?

If it's less than a 30 min drive, he would go visit. Use Google maps and the conditional operator to help him make a decision if he want to go or to stay home.

https://goo.gl/maps/wJwU9

YOUR CODE:

```
1
2
3
4
5
6
7
8
```

ANSWER:

Are blocks of code *repeated* number of times

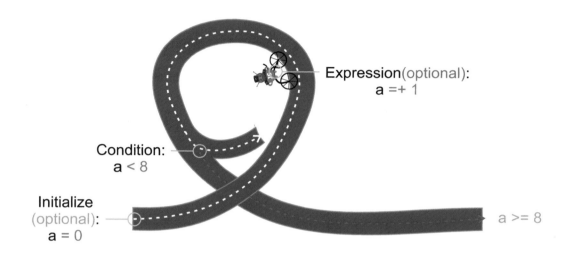

Expression(optional):
a =+ 1

Condition:
a < 8

Initialize
(optional):
a = 0

a >= 8

Private JS will loop 7 times, then it will proceed on the red path

while

```
1    //requires a condition to run
2    //at least once
3    while (var a < 8) {
4        alert(a);
5        a += 1;
6    }
```

for

```
1    //add 1 to "a" until "a" is no longer less than 8
2    //initialize; condition; expression
3    for (var a = 0; a < 8; a = a + 1) {
4        alert(a);
5    }
6    //if "a" is equal or greater than 8, go here
```

for in

```
1    var fruit = {a: "kiwi", b: "pear", c: "fig"};
2    //go through the properties of an object
3    for (var o in fruit) {
4            //test for property's existence
5        if (fruit.hasOwnProperty(o)) {
6            alert(fruit[o]);
7        }
8    }
9    //not recommended for arrays
```

do while

```
1    //runs at least once before
2    //meeting the condition
3    do {
4        alert(a);
5        a += 1;
6    }
7    while (a < 8);
```

43. EXERCISE:
Loops.

PROBLEM:

Print the numbers 11 to 23 separated by a comma in the document window.

Don't worry about the last comma yet.

YOUR CODE:

```
1
2
3
4
5
6
7
8
```

ANSWER:

Are variables that can store *multiple values*

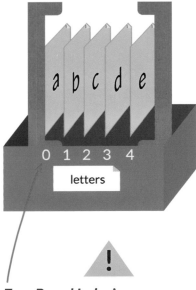

Zero Based Indexing:
[0] is the first element (a),
[1] is the second element (b),
[2] is the third element (c)...

With the help of pair of brackets I can store multiple values in one variable

```
1    //define an array
2    var letters = ['a', 'b', 'c', 'd','e'];
3    //return the length of the array
4    console.log(letters.length);     //5
5    //return the second element
6    console.log(letters[1]);          //b
```

```
1    //create an array of numbers
2    var letters = [1, 2, 3, 4];
```

Arrays are flexible and can contain:
Objects, Functions, Other Arrays

```
1    //get the first element
2    var name = letters[0];     //1
```

```
1    //set the second element
2    letters[1] = "String";    //2 changed
3    //[1, "String", 3, 4]
```

45.EXERCISE:
Arrays.

PROBLEM:

Create an array of 5 numbers (1 to 5)
Change the first element to your name.
Change the last element with your 3 favorite colors.

YOUR CODE:

```
1
2
3
4
5
6
7
8
```

ANSWER:

Array objects have *predefined* methods

shift, unshift
as **sh**amrock green

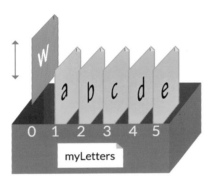

```
1    //define an array
2    var myLetters = ['a', 'b', 'c', 'd'];
3
4    //add at the beginning
5    myLetters.unshift('w');
6    // ['w', 'a', 'b', 'c', 'd'];
7
8    //remove the first
9    myLetters.shift('w');
10   // ['a', 'b', 'c', 'd'];
```

push, pop
as **p**eriod **p**urple

```
1    //define an array
2    var myLetters = ['a', 'b', 'c', 'd'];
3
4    //add to the end
5    myLetters.push('w');
6    // ['a', 'b', 'c', 'd', 'w'];
7
8    //remove the last element
9    myLetters.pop('w');
10   // ['a', 'b', 'c', 'd'];
```

PROBLEM:

Use a loop to create an array containing the numbers 11 to 23.
Display the numbers on the screen

YOUR CODE:

```
1
2
3
4
5
6
7
8
```

ANSWER:

Functions (Fun actions) are groups of code that can be *called later*

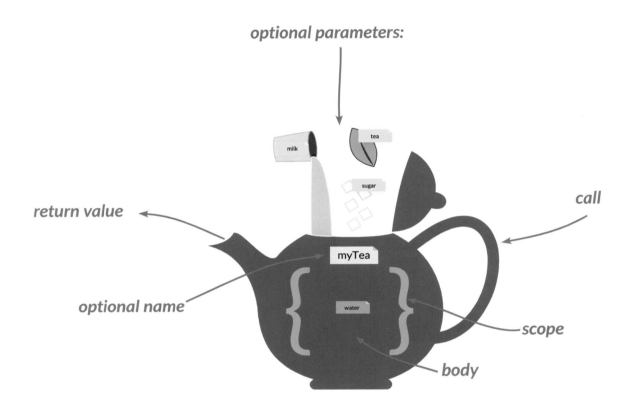

optional parameters:

return value

call

optional name

scope

body

The function of a teapot is to prepare and serve tea

```
1   //Define a function that makes tea
2   //Functions are objects and can be assigned to variables:
3
4   //Pass parameters "tea", "sugar" and "milk" to the function:
5   var myTea = function(tea, sugar, milk) {
6       var water = "Hot water, ";           //water is a private variable, invisible outside of the function
7       return water + tea + ", " + sugar + " sugars" + ", " + milk + " milks";
8   };
9
10  //Call the function with custom parameters
11  myTea("green tea", 2, 3);
12  //Hot water, green tea, 2 sugars, 3 milks
```

PROBLEM:

Make a function 'cm2in' that converts CM(centimeters) to IN(inches). Round the result with Math.round() and add the inch symbol (") after the value

RESULT:

6"

YOUR CODE:

```
1
2
3
4
5
6
7
8
```

ANSWER:

Enclosing of code blocks into one another

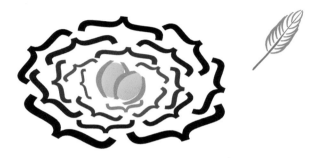

Avoid deep nesting when possible, because it slows down the script and can be confusing to other programmers

```
1    //functions nesting
2    function one() {
3        function two() {
4            function three() {
5        return 1;
6            }
7      return 2;
8        }
9     return 3;
10   }
11
12   //if statements nesting
13    if (true) {
14      if (true) {
15        if (true) {
16                true;
17        } else {
18            false;
19        }
20      } else {
21          false;
22      }
23    } else {
24        false;
25    }
```

51. EXERCISE:
Nesting.

PROBLEM:

Fix the error in the nested 'if else' statement

```
1    if (true) {
2        return 1;
3    } else {
4        return 0;
5    }
⊘ 6    Syntax Error
```

YOUR CODE:

```
1
2
3
4
5
6
7
8
```

ANSWER:

All HTML elements and attributes are *nodes* in the Document Object Model (DOM)

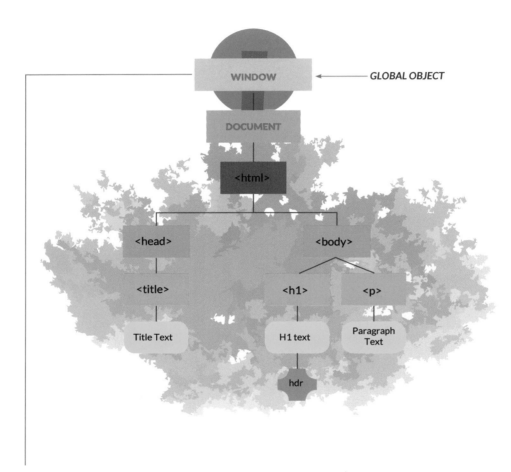

Each tab has its own window object

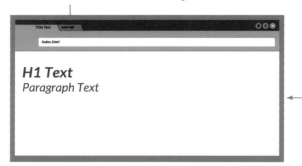

HTML representation of the DOM

```
1  <html>
2    <head>
3      <title>Title Text</title>
4    </head>
5    <body>
6      <h1 id="hdr">H1 Text</h1>
7      <p>Paragraph Text</p>
8    </body>
9  </html>
```
index.html

PROBLEM:

Draw a node tree diagram representing the following HTML

```
1  <html>
2    <head>
3        <title>Draw me</title>
4    </head>
5    <body>
6        <h1 id="hdr">Hello</h1>
7        <h2>Header tag</h2>
8        <p id ="para">My text</p>
9        <script src = "my.js"></script>
10   </body>
11</html>
```
index.html

YOUR DIAGRAM:

ANSWER:

JavaScript is used to manipulate the content of HTML elements (the DOM)

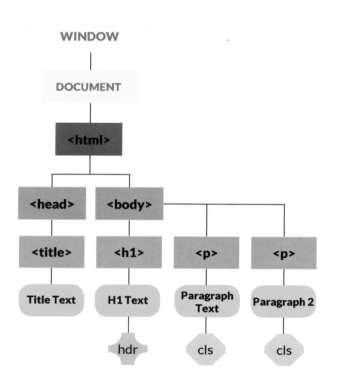

```
1  <html>
2    <head>
3      <title>Title Text</title>
4    </head>
5    <body>
6      <h1 id="hdr">H1 Text</h1>
7      <p class="cls">Paragraph Text</p>
8      <p class="cls">Paragraph 2</p>
9      <script src = "main.js"></script>
10   </body>
11 </html>
                                    index.html
```

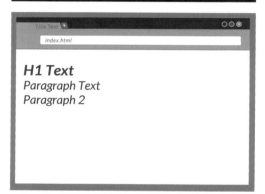

```
1   //returns all elements with the id "hdr"
2   getId = document.getElementById("hdr");
3   //<h1 id="hdr">H1 Text</h1>
4
5   //returns a node collection of all p tags
6   console.log(document.getElementsByTagName("p"));
7   //[p.cls, p.cls, item: function]
8
9   //returns all elements with the class name "cls"
10  console.log(document.getElementsByClassName("cls"));
11  //[p.cls, p.cls, item: function]
12
13  //Modify the content of the h1 element with the innerHTML property
14  getId.innerHTML = "Something Else";
15  //<h1 id="hdr">Something Else</h1>
                                                      main.js
```

55.EXERCISE:
Manipulating the DOM.

PROBLEM:

Select the <p> tag with id **"cls"** and change the text to "something else"

```
1  <html>
2   <head>
3    <title>Draw me</title>
4   </head>
5    <body>
6     <h1 id="hdr">Hello</h1>
7     <h2>Header tag</h2>
8     <p id="cls">Paragraph 2</p>
9     <script src = "my.js"></script>
10   </body>
11 </html>
```

YOUR CODE:

```
1
2
3
4
5
6
7
8
```

ANSWER:

```
item = group[ (current.index + 1 ) % len ];
```

coming.c

F._after

Function statement is where a *statement begins* with the word "function".
If not, it's a function *expression*.

```
1    //Functions are values
2
3    //function Statements (Declarations) require a name,
4
5    //are defined at parse time and
6    //can be called before being declared because of hoisting
7    foo();
8    function foo() { return 8; }
```

*there is nothing before
the word "function", so it's a statement*

> *I prefer the function expressions, because
> they are more flexible*

```
1    //function Expression.
2    //name is optional
3    //defined at run time
4    var foo = function foo() { return 8; };
5    foo();      //8
6
7    //function Expression with parameters
8    var boo = function (x, y) { return x + y; };
9    boo(2,3); //5
10
11   //anonymous function Expression
12   var moo = function() { return 1; };
13   moo();   //1
14
15   //this is a function Expression
16   //because it is inside a grouping operator ()
17   ( function doo() { return 8; }() );
18   //8
```

*this is an expression because of the assignment
operator*

*the grouping operator can only contain an
expression*

57.EXERCISE:
Function Statements vs Function Expressions.

PROBLEM:

In JavaScript we can raise a number to a power with the Math.pow(x,y) method. X is the base and Y the exponent.
Refactor the following function and make it a function expression:

```
1   //raise the number 2 to the power of 10
2   function power(x) {
3       //not very nice. Let's rewrite
4       var raise= x*x*x*x*x*x*x*x*x*x + x;        // (x^{10})
5       return raise;
6   }
7   power(2);
8   //1026
```

YOUR CODE:

```
1
2
3
4
5
6
```

ANSWER:

```
item = group[ (current.index + i ) % len ];
```
coming.c
F._after

IIFEs are self-executing functions that are used to avoid variable hoisting and to protect the global space from 'polluting'

```
1    //we will never call it, so no need for a name
2    ( function () {
3        console.log("no need to call me");
4    }() );
5    //The second pair of parentheses at the end invokes the function
```

```
1    var x = function() {
2        console.log("no need to call me");
3    }();
4    //The second pair of parentheses at the end calls and closes the function
5    //if we try to call it later, we get an error:
6    x();
7    TypeError: undefined is not a function
```

Anything that will force the interpreter to evaluate whatever comes next, will invoke the function

```
1    //Any of the following can do the job:
2    //+, -, ~, !, void, true, &&, new
3    !function () {
4        console.log("no need to call me");
5    }();
6    //true
7
8    +function () {        //try to convert to a number
9        console.log("no need to call me");
10   }();
11   //NaN
12
13   0, function () {
14       console.log("no need to call me");
15   }();
16   //undefined
```

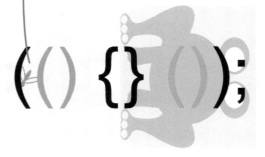

Remember the mirror frog pattern

PROBLEM:

Add no more than 4 characters to make this function self-executing:

```
1    function selfExecute() {
2        console.log("Make me IIFE, please!");
3    }
```

YOUR CODE:

```
1
2
3
4
5
6
7
8
```

ANSWER:

60.Scope.

JavaScript has function-level scope. Variables inside a function are invisible to the outside.
The *local scope* can "see" the global scope, but the *global scope* can't "see" the local scope.

variable inside a function

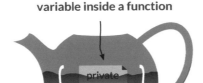

private

Local Scope

function

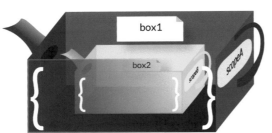

Nested functions

variable outside a function

public

Global Scope

```
1    //global variable is a variable
2    //outside a function
3    var public = "pink";
```

```
1    var private = "white";              //global scope
2    //same variable name inside and outside a function
3    //is called a "shadowed" variable
4    function shadow() {
5        var private = "orange";          //local var
6        console.log(private);            //orange
7    //'window' and 'this' have access to the global scope
8        console.log(window.private);     //white
9        console.log(this.private);       //white
10   }
11   shadow();
```

Scope chain (nested functions)

```
1    var box = 1;          //global scope
2    function scopeA() {
3        var box1 = 2;
4        console.log(box1);
5            function scopeB() {
6                var box2 = 4;
7                console.log(box2+box1+box);
8            }
9        scopeB();
10   }
11
12   scopeA();
13   //2
14   //7
```

```
1    //variable without the 'var' keyword
2    //is a global variable
3    function shadow() {
4        public = "blue";      //no 'var' keyword
5    }
```

```
1    //if... statements have braces,
2    //but do not create new scope, only functions do
3    if (true) {
4        var global = "blue";
5    }
```

61.EXERCISE:
Scope.

PROBLEM:

The function below is suppose to count 10 apples.
Fix the problem!

```
1    var i = "red";
2
3    function countApples() {
4        for (i; i <= 10; i++) {
5            console.log(i);
6        }
7    }
8    countApples();
```

YOUR CODE:

```
1
2
3
4
5
6
7
8
```

ANSWER:

Function and variable declarations are moved *to the top* of their scope

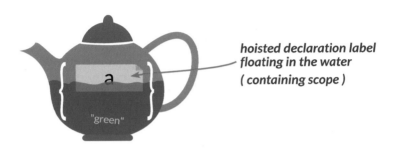

hoisted declaration label
floating in the water
(containing scope)

variable hoisting

```
1    //variable declarations are moved to
2    //the top. Only the declarations!
3    function hoistedVar() {
4        alert(a);
5        var a = "green";
6        alert(a);
7    }
8    hoistedVar();
9    //undefined
10   //green
```

function hoisting

```
1    // Let's call a function before it is defined
2    declaration();
3    // function name and definitions
4    // are moved to the top.
5    function declaration() {
6        alert("function declaration called");
7    }
8    //function declaration called
```

```
1    //the above will be interpreted like this:
2    function hoistedVar() {
3        var a;              //the hoisted variable
4        alert(a);           //undefined
5        var a = "green";
6        alert(a);           //green
7    }
8    hoistedVar();
```

```
1    // function expressions are not hoisted
2    expression();
3    var expression = function() {
4        alert("function expression not called");
5    };
⊗6   TypeError: undefined is not a function
```

63.EXERCISE:
Hoisting.

PROBLEM:

What is the result of the following code ? Why ?
Try to answer without running the code.

```
1    test();
2    var test = function () {
3        return 1;
4    };
```

YOUR ANSWER:

1
2
3

ANSWER:

Functions that have access to *upper* function variables and parameters even after the execution of the upper function. It *"closes over"* the free variables (variables outside the function)

innerFn remembers the environment in which it was created

InnerFn has access to the global scope too

X and Z are free variables to innerFn

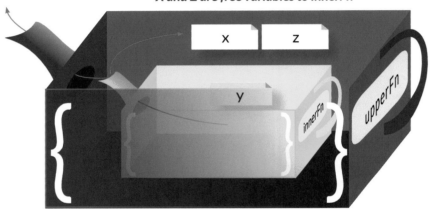

Nested functions

Variable 'z' survived the upper function execution

```
1    function upperFn(x) {
2      var z = 8;    //local variable
3
4    //closure is formed during function instantiation, not during invocation
5        function innerFn(y) {        //closure
6            console.log(x + y + z);
7      }
8        innerFn(3);                  //y = 3
9    }
10   upperFn(2);                      //x = 2
11
12   //13
13   //When 'upperFn' is called, function 'innerFn'
14   //is instantiated and has access to variable 'z'
```

65.EXERCISE:
Closures.

PROBLEM:

Make a function with parameter x that returns a function with parameter y which returns the sum of x and y.

console.log the sum of 3 and 5

YOUR CODE:

```
1
2
3
```

ANSWER:

When to run methods (*event*ually)

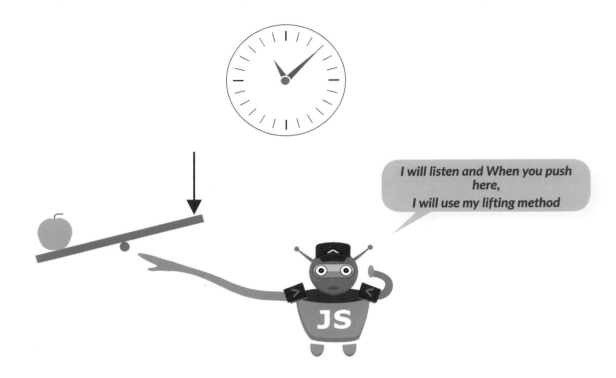

element.event = function;

```
1    //When mouse is clicked on a text
2    <p onclick="this.innerHTML='YES'">Click Me</p>
3
4    //When you click a button, pop-up a message
5    <button onclick="alert('Thanks')">Click Me</button>
6
7    //Better way to execute events, note the semicolon at the end
8    document.onclick = function() { alert ("I was clicked"); };
9
10   //Best way to execute events, but beware IE old versions
11   document.addEventListener ('click', myFunction() {alert("wow"); } );
```

PROBLEM:

Create an event listener that calculates a button clicks and displays that number on the screen

```
1  <html>
2    <head>
3        <title>Click me</title>
4        <p id="hdr">0</p>
5        <button onclick = "countClicks();">Click!</button>
6    </head>
7      <body>
8        <script src = "my.js"></script>
9      </body>
10 </html>
```

YOUR CODE:

```
1
2
3
4
5
6
7
8
```

ANSWER:

Objects are collections of properties and methods. In JavaScript everything is an object.

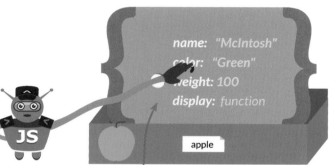

I can use the "Dot Notation" to Get or Set a property or a method

```
object.property;
object.method;
```

name: "McIntosh"
color: "Green"
weight: 100
display: function

apple

Think of the 'dot notation' as an opening in the object to access his content

```
1    //create an empty object
2    var apple = {};
3
4    //create an object and add properties to it
5    var apple = {
6        name: "McIntosh",
7        color: "Green",
8        weight: 100,
9        //add method
10       display: function () { alert("I weigh " + this.weight + "g");}
11   };
```

this means current object

set

```
1    //property change with "." dot notation
2    apple.color = "Red";
3    //add the new smell property
4    apple.smell = "Fresh";
```

get

```
1    //call the method of the apple object
2    apple.display();
3    //result: I weigh 100 g
4    //get the value of a property
5    var getValue = apple.weight;
```

apple

name: "McIntosh"
smell : "Fresh"
color: "Red"

weight: 100
display: function

set ⟶ get

69.EXERCISE:
Objects.

PROBLEM: Create an object literal containing the details of this vehicle's registration form. Delete Year of Manufacture and display the object in the console

Owners Name:	John Smith
Chasis No.:	451265-458
Engine No.:	6565-5656-98
Make Name:	Stealth
Registration Date:	1 July 2019
Vehicle Price:	$145 000
Color:	Burgundy
Year of Manufacture:	2018

YOUR CODE:

```
1
2
3
4
5
6
7
8
9
10
11
12
13
```

ANSWER:

Are *functions* associated with an object

Methods are things for Me To Do

Methods to lift an object

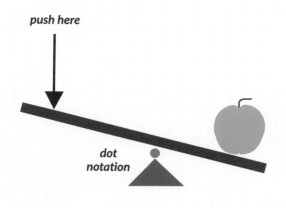

push here

dot
notation

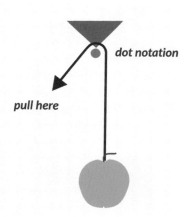

dot notation

pull here

```
1    var apple = {          //object
2        lift: function() {    //method
3            alert ('lift an object');
4        }
5    };
```

```
1    //call the method
2    apple.lift();
3    //perform the action "lift" on the "apple" object.
4    //use a dot motation to call the method
5    //object [dot] method
```

71.EXERCISE:
Methods.

PROBLEM:

JavaScript has some predefined methods such as 'toUpperCase()' to convert lowercase strings to uppercase.

Use it to convert your name to uppercase.

YOUR CODE:

```
1
2
3
4
5
6
7
8
```

ANSWER:

Are functions used to create multiple instances of an object using the **'*new*'** keyword

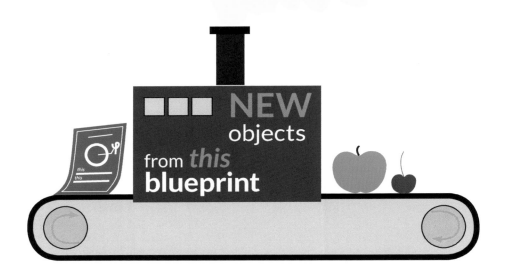

```
1    //Constructor functions start with a capital letter by convention
2
3    var Fruit = function Fruit(name, color) {
4        this.name = name;        //property
5        this.color= color;
6        //method
7        this.info = function() { return "I am a " + this.color + " " + this.name };
8    }
9
10   //Now we can easily create a large number of instances of the same object:
11   //keyword 'new' sets the context of 'this' to the newly created object
12   var Cherry = new Fruit();
13   var Apple = new Fruit();
14   var Mango = new Fruit();
```

PROBLEM:

Fix the following code:

```
1    var user = function (name) {
2        this.name = name;
3    };
4    var john = user("John");
```

YOUR CODE:

```
1
2
3
4
5
6
7
8
```

ANSWER:

Every function has a property called 'prototype'.
It allows to add properties and methods to objects, so they can share information easier.

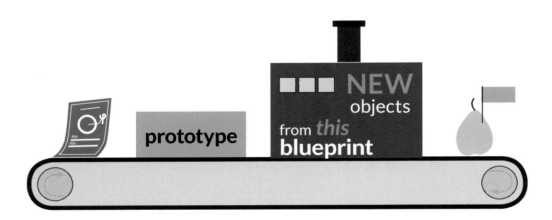

Prototypes allow you to define properties and methods to all instances of a particular object

```
1   //Constructor function
2   var Fruit = function Fruit(name, color) {
3       this.name = name;
4       this.color = color;
5       this.info = function() { return 'I am a ' + this.color + ' ' + this.name; };
6   }
7
8   //let's add a property to the Fruit prototype object
9   Fruit.prototype.price = 100;
10  //and a new method
11  Fruit.prototype.cost = function() { return 'This ' + this.name + ' costs ' + this.price; };
12
13  //now let's create a new instance of Fruit
14  var pear = new Fruit('pear', 'golden');
15  console.log(pear.price);
16  //100
17  console.log(pear.info());
18  //I am a golden pear
19  console.log(pear.cost());
20  //This pear costs 100
```

PROBLEM:

The following constructor counts the amount of instances it has.
Fix the code to make it work properly

```
1   var Counter = function() {
2       this.count++;
3   };
4   Counter.prototype.count = 0;
5   new Counter();
6   new Counter();
7   console.log((new Counter() ).count);    //should be 3
```

YOUR CODE:

```
1
2
3
4
5
6
7
8
```

ANSWER:

CPSIA information can be obtained at www.ICGtesting.com
Printed in the USA
LVIW01n2046261115
464315LV00022B/282